BOKER TOV

A CULINARY LOVE STORY
FROM TEL AVIV

TOM SAS
LORI DARDIKMAN

Lannoo

BOKERTOV GOEDEN

صباح الخير GUTEN

BOM DIA G

HYVÄÄ HUOMENTA コ

BOKERTOV GOEDEN

صباح الخير GUTEN

BOM DIA G

HYVÄÄ HUOMENTA コ

BOKERTOV GOEDEN

صباح الخير GUTEN

BOM DIA G

HYVÄ Ä HUOMENTA

RGEN GOODMORNING

MORGEN BUENOS DÍAS

NAYDIN GOD MORGEN

בוקר ט BUON GIORNO

RGEN GOODMORNING

MORGEN BUENOS DÍAS

NAYDIN GOD MORGEN

בוקר ט BUON GIORNO

RGEN GOODMORNING

MORGEN BUENOS DÍAS

NAYDIN GOD MORGEN

בוקר ט BUON GIORNO

INDEX

SHALOM	17
A LOVE STORY	20
BOKER TOV	23
SHABBAT - IT'S A FAMILY AFFAIR	27
THE SCENTS AND COLOURS OF SHUK HACARMEL	28
SPICES AND SEASONINGS	33
BASIC PREPARATIONS	43
BREAD	55
BREAKFAST	65
TO SHARE	83
BIG BITES	119
SWEETS	143
DRINKS	163
TEL AVIV	173
LAILA TOV	181
TODA RABA	185

SPICES AND SEASONINGS 32
RAS EL HANOUT 36
ZA'ATAR 36
DUKAH 37
MUSTARD SEEDS 37
POMEGRANATE MOLASSES 40
SILAN 40
HARISSA 41
PRESERVED LEMONS 41

BASIC PREPARATIONS 42
BRINE FOR FRUITS AND VEGETABLES 44
CHICKEN BOUILLON 44
YUZU VINAIGRETTE 45
PICKLED GREEN PEPPERS 45
OLIVES 46
LABNEH 46
CHARIF 47
TAHINI 47
MISOTAHINI 50
AMBA 50
GREEN ZHUG 51
RED ZHUG 51
HUMMUS 52

BREAD 54
BAGELS 56
CHALLAH 59
ZA'ATAR FLATBREAD 62
LAFFA 63

BREAKFAST 64
SHAKSHUKA 66
ZA'ATAR EGGS 69
FUL 70
GRANOLA 71
FRENCH TOAST 72
BOREKAS 75
TEL AVIV CROQUE MADAME 76
PICKLED SALMON 79
POACHED EGGS WITH LABNEH AND 80
ALEPPO PEPPER BUTTER

TO SHARE 82
FATTOUSH SALAD 89
TABBOULEH 90
BARBECUED AUBERGINES 93
SEABASS CEVICHE WITH SUMAC AND 94
PUL BIBER

AUTUMN HUMMUS WITH STEWED 98
MUSHROOMS
WINTERHUMMUS WITH BARBECUE 100
VEGETABLES
SPRING HUMMUS WITH MINCED MEAT 101
AND PINE NUTS
SUMMER HUMMUS WITH EGG AND 102
TOMATO SALAD
TA'AMEYA (EGYPTIAN FALAFEL) 105
BOKER TOV CHICKEN SCHNITZEL 106
COLESLAW 110
ROASTED CARROTS WITH CHERMOULA 110
AND HARISSA
COURGETTE AND BURRATA SALAD 113
CELERIAC WITH GOAT CHEESE AND 116
GRILLED GRAPES
PTITIM – ISRAELI COUSCOUS 117

BIG BITES 118
CHICKEN SCHNITZEL & COLESLAW IN 120
LEBANESE BREAD
PASTRAMI SANDWICH 123
SABICH 124
FLOWER POWER CAULIFLOWER 127
TELADOG 130
CHRAIME WITH COURGETTES 133
BARBECUED SEA BREAM WITH MANY 134
SIDE DISHES
CHOLENT WITH OXTAIL 137

SWEETS 142
ARRACK CRÈME BRÛLÉE 145
FRIED RICE PUDDING 146
TAHINI BROWNIES 149
MALABI 150
ORANGE TART WITH CARDAMOM 153
SWEET CHALLAH WITH FIGS AND 154
HONEY LABNEH
HAZELNUT CAKE WITH LABNEH 155
AND PLUMS
MANGO SORBET WITH LABNEH AND 156
NUT & POPPY SNAPS
BABKA CAKE 159

DRINKS 150
LIMONANA 164
VERVEINE ICED TEA 167
ISRAELI PORNSTAR 168
SUMAGRONI 171

SHALOM

Shalom!

My father was born in Tel Aviv in 1954. In his youth, he often skipped school to go play Matkot on the beach, together with his friends. So, his days were mostly filled with carefree fun. My grandmother, Aviva, was an excellent cook. She prepared his favorite dish Chollent deliciously, and we are pleased to say that this dish has been a great inspiration for Orlando, chef at the Laila restaurant. During family gatherings, this dish is often still served. Pure nostalgia!

When becoming older he discovered the high energy nightlife of Tel Aviv. After going out, his best friend Gershon and he always ended the night (or morning) in an eatery, finishing a plate of hummus or even Chipudim (a barbecue goose liver & lamb brochette) before going home. After fulfilling the military service, he came to Antwerp to discover another vibrant city and study diamonds. He learned how to sort them and find the best quality. And that's where he sourced his most valuable diamond, Marianne, my mother. He came to Antwerp for business but stayed for love.

I was always fascinated by my father's stories about Tel Aviv; they pushed me to go and discover the high energy city myself. What started as a short trip, ended up being a journey of almost three years. I lived there, worked there, and was completely immersed in a new city. After this adventure, I decided to go back to my family in Antwerp, but Tel Aviv was always in my heart.

When I met Tom, my parents were a little skeptical about him (and all his tattoos) at first. But once they got to know him, my family embraced him. It was definitely a plus that he and abba shared the same passion for good food and drinks. Together with Tom, I was able to bring my love for Tel Aviv to Antwerp. It makes me immensely proud to see what we have accomplished together.

Wherever I go, people compliment me about Boker Tov: about the food, about the enthusiastic team. If even my Tel Avivian friends feel at home and sense the atmosphere of Tel Aviv in Boker Tov... why shouldn't you?

Beteavon! Smakelijk!

Lori

A LOVE STORY

When two people with a shared passion for good food and Tel Aviv meet, the result is fireworks. This is precisely what happened to Tom Sas and Lori Dardikman, the owners of Boker Tov.

LORI

Although Lori's father is from Tel Aviv, she had never visited the city as a child. At the age of twenty, she decided it was time to travel around the world. Her dream was to go to Thailand, but she ended up spending a holiday with her aunt in Tel Aviv.

Lori fell in love with the city from day one. She was charmed by the magnificent buildings and the beautiful weather. But it was the hospitality, the warmth and the friendliness of the inhabitants in particular that convinced her to stay.

She missed the plane home on purpose and went looking for work and a place to live. Not that life in Tel Aviv was easy. It was hard work to pay the rent. Her shift at a coffee shop ran from 6 a.m. to 2 p.m. From 2 p.m. to 8 p.m. she au paired for twins before working late into the night in a La Chouffe bar. It may surprise you, but La Chouffe, like many other Belgian beers, is very popular in Israel. Lori was convinced that, no matter what happened, she would always have a bed, food and work in the city. And on Saturdays, shabbat (sabbath in English), she was always welcome somewhere for a shabbat meal.

The planned two-week holiday turned into two years. And Lori had lost her heart to Tel Aviv forever.

TOM

Meanwhile in Belgium, Tom Sas was building a career in the hospitality industry. After starting as an assistant bartender at a restaurant in Zoersel, his boss quickly realized that Tom had a special talent for welcoming people. On weekends he earned his living at discotheque La Rocca, during the week as hospitality manager for restaurants, events and festivals. He worked alongside great chefs like Sergio Herman at festivals such as We Can Dance and Tomorrowland, opened the pop-up Butcher Bar in the South of Antwerp and created Karavaan Streetcatering from zero.

Although Tom rarely visited restaurants as a child, the decadence of fine dining immediately attracted him. Birthdays were invariably celebrated with best friends Nico and Thierry, with the birthday boy choosing the restaurant and the others paying. He gained a nose for good food and star restaurants, as well as the street stall with the best hot dogs, fries or falafel.

Tel Aviv was not unknown to him. He got to know the city on a city trip and fell in love immediately. The 24/24 vibe, the mix of cultures and religions, the fantastic food, the beautiful weather... It was a city of extremes in which he felt very much himself. The visit convinced him that one day he wanted to do something related to Tel Aviv in Antwerp.

TOM & LORI

In 2016, Tomorrowland changed beer sponsor. Tom was asked to take care of the hospitality part of the Brew District. He accepted the challenge enthusiastically, convinced that his extensive network would come in handy. The project became the absolute place to be at the festival providing fine wining and dining, as well as a swimming pool, massage parlour and barbershop.

Lori was the Brew District host and made sure all guests were welcomed with open arms. Her attractive appearance and charming, easy-going personality made everyone feel welcome. Tom also noticed that and the two soon started talking. For them it's a bit over the top to talk of love at first sight, but nevertheless, sparks flew during their first conversation—enough to have them move in together after the festival. After an intense festival summer, their bond was so strong that they started dreaming of a future together.

We are now six years down the line and Tom and Lori have two beautiful daughters together—Milla aged four and Liya aged two. Their family also includes Ben (11), Tom's son from a previous relationship. In addition to their family life, they run five restaurants together. This creates a continuous and pleasant busyness, making them feel at times like they're in Tel Aviv. Their Sundays in particular are generally totally balagan...

CHAIM SHELI MY LIFE, MY LOVE

BOKER TOV

The story of a restaurant usually starts with a chef who finds a place where he can open a restaurant and then comes up with a concept. Not so at Boker Tov.

Inspired by Tel Aviv's hospitality and culinary vibe, Lori and Tom were keen on bringing a piece of the city to Antwerp. It was not immediately clear how they would do this. Would it be window sales in a busy city location where people could grab a quick bite? Would it be a small bar? A hip food truck? All possibilities were open. In any case, it would not be a traditional restaurant, with lunch served from noon and dinner from 6 p.m. The couple instinctively sensed that people were ready for something new, a place with an all-day buzz, adapted to the rhythm of contemporary life.

When the coffee bar that they regularly visited closed its doors after the first lockdown, everything suddenly accelerated. Tom had been looking for a place for an office for some time. He also wanted to receive visitors there and, if possible, it had to include a kitchen to provide the home base for Karavaan Streetfood Catering. The property on Doornelei met all the criteria. Even before the contract was properly signed, the couple set to work. The property turned out to be so spacious that there was even room for a restaurant.

Tom and Lori would have preferred to be open 24 hours a day. Unfortunately, Belgian wage costs make that impossible. A restaurant serving delicious Middle Eastern dishes seven days a week was the alternative.

They had a list of names, but in the end, it became Boker Tov. That's 'good morning' in Hebrew, but can also be interpreted more broadly as 'welcome' or 'have a nice day'. Tom and Lori translated it as 'catch your best moment of the day'. Boker Tov had to be a place where everyone feels at home and can taste the no-nonsense Middle Eastern cuisine that Ottolenghi and others have since made popular.

PLEASE DO NOT ENTER IF YOU HAVE ANY SYMPTOMS OF COVID 19, RACISM OR HOMOPHOBIA

ANTWERP MEETS TEL AVIV

Boker Tov was right on target from day one. People lined up on the pavement to get a table. Every seat was continuously occupied. Barely four days after its opening, the restaurant had to close its doors due to the second corona wave. Having invested their last cents in Boker Tov, Tom and Lori had to move fast. They came up with a take-away concept—*the balagan box*—which became an instant hit. *Balagan* means 'cozy mess' in Hebrew, and in this case a lot of tasty snacks. With the box you can conjure up a table full of delicious dishes in just over fifteen minutes. All you need is an oven.

Thomas Swenters, a young chef who earned his spurs in De Librije and the Upper Room Bar at The Jane, soon joined the adventure. He had a great feel for the concept and understood the cuisine Tom and Lori had in mind like none other. By giving it his own twist, he helped make Boker Tov a success.

Through social media and with the help of a strong community, things quickly shifted into higher gear. The formula worked so well that Tom and Lori opened a second restaurant in Antwerp's former harbour area Het Eilandje during full lockdown. A year after the first opening, a smaller delivery-focused business came into being on the Eiermarkt.

Boker Tov is open seven days a week from 8 a.m. to 8 p.m. People come here in the morning to quietly read the newspaper with a cup of coffee while enjoying a sandwich, a steaming plate of *shakshuka* or a full-scale meal. The dishes are kosher—often vegetarian or vegan— and served all day long.

In August 2021, Boker Tov got a big sister, Laila (which means 'night' in Hebrew). A hip rooftop restaurant on the ninth floor of an office building on the Mechelsesteenweg with fine dining, dirty dancing and a fantastic view over Antwerp.

With this book, Tom and Lori introduce an even wider audience to Tel Aviv. The recipes, by Thomas Swenters, show you how to prepare your own *balagan*—a glorious chaos of fantastic dishes that you share with as many people as possible.

Beteavon!

SHABBAT

IT'S A FAMILY AFFAIR

Shabbat (sabbath) is celebrated in a variety of ways, differing from one family to another, but ultimately, it's about being together. *Shabbat* starts at sunset on Friday and lasts until sunset on Saturday. That's twenty-four hours, but in most cases *shabbat* actually refers to a meal.

On *shabbat* you are supposed to abstain from work—and thus from cooking—but it doesn't require you to be frugal or to fast. In preparation, families bring lots of good food into the house. *Challah* bread, for example, should not be missing. Stews simmer on the stove long in advance and friends and family are invited for dinner. At Lori's house, *chraime* and *cholent* are a regular part of the meal. The whole family shares not only the bread, but also their experiences with each other.

It's no different in Tel Aviv. After dinner with the family, the young people go out and interpret the old Torah customs more flexibly. Yet, being together remains of the essence throughout the day.

THE SCENTS AND COLOURS OF SHUK HACARMEL

THE SHUK

Shuk HaCarmel or Carmel Market is a regular part of Tom and Lori's visits to Tel Aviv. The market is open every day (except Saturdays, *shabbat*) from 7 in the morning until dusk.

Nowhere else in the world will you find such an explosion of colours, smells and flavours. Stall-lined streets offer a huge variety of fresh fruits and vegetables, piled high in colourful heaps. Large containers offer wonderfully fragrant spices in warm shades of ochre, yellow and brown. The scent of warm, fresh-baked bread hangs in the air. Here you will find almost every herb on earth and can buy the freshest fish and the tastiest meat.

Nowhere else are your senses stimulated as much as in this *shuk*. Pleasantly busy all day long, Shuk HaCarmel can be overwhelming on a first visit. But once you get to appreciate the hustle and bustle, you return to find more than you came looking for.

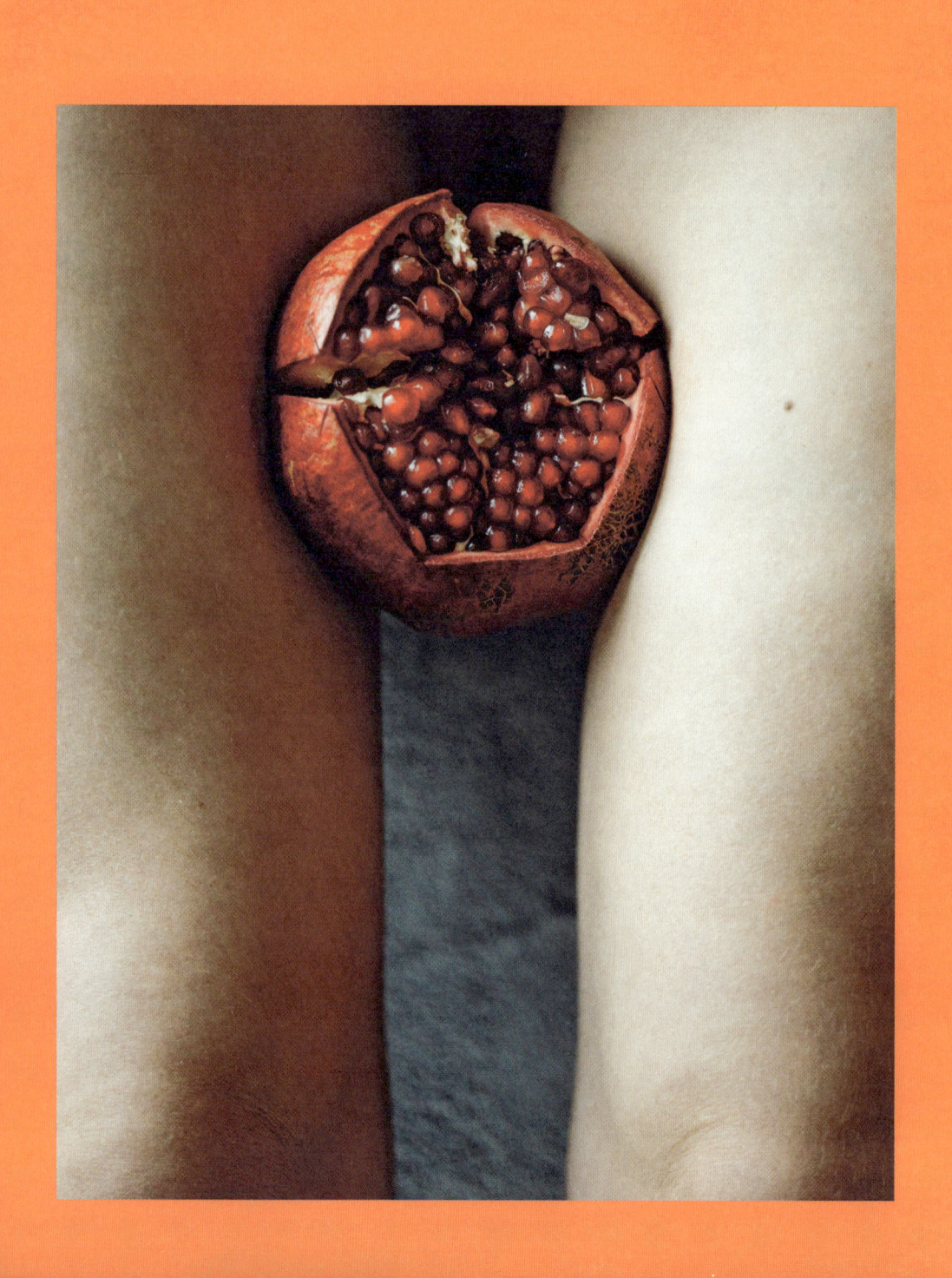

SPICES AND SEASONINGS

RAS EL HANOUT

Ras el hanout literally means 'the best of the store'. You can buy it ready-made, but you can also make your own custom mixture. This is the recipe we use at Boker Tov, but feel free to experiment with the flavours you like best.

INGREDIENTS

1.5 tsp coriander seed
1 tsp cumin seed
½ tsp *pul biber* (flakes from Aleppo pepper)
1 tsp cinnamon powder
1 tsp paprika powder
½ tsp cardamom powder
½ tsp ginger powder
½ tsp turmeric powder
¼ tsp clove powder
¼ tsp allspice
1 tsp rose petals

PREPARATION

Toast the coriander seeds and cumin seeds in a non-stick pan without oil until fragrant. Place all the spices in a mortar and grind fine. Last of all, mix in the rose petals.

Store the *ras el hanout* in a cool, dry place in a tightly closed jar.

ZA'ATAR

When Lori lived in Tel Aviv, she often went walking on Saturdays in a park just outside the city. At the park entrance sat a woman selling simple, freshly baked *laffa* (type of flatbread) with *labneh* and *za'atar*. Although Lori normally didn't care for *labneh*, those flatbreads were the best she had ever tasted. *Za'atar* is available ready-made in the store, but the quality is not always good. You can easily make your own with spices and herbs that you may already have in your pantry.

INGREDIENTS

1 tbsp dried oregano
1 tbsp sumac
1 tbsp white sesame seeds
1 tbsp cumin powder
1 tsp salt
1 tsp white pepper from the mill

PREPARATION

Mix the oregano with the sumac, sesame seeds, cumin powder, salt and white pepper.

Store the *za'atar* in a cool, dry place in a tightly closed jar.

DUKKAH

This crunchy mixture of nuts and spices is widely used in Middle Eastern cuisine. You sprinkle it over all kinds of dishes or use it to make a *crunchy* dip.

INGREDIENTS

50 g peeled hazelnuts
50 g almonds with skin
1.5 tsp cumin powder
1 tbsp coriander powder
1 tbsp sesame seeds
1 tbsp salt
1 tsp paprika powder
1 tsp *za'atar*
1 tsp fennel seeds
1 tsp sumac
1 tsp turmeric powder

PREPARATION

Preheat the oven to 180°C. Place the hazelnuts and almonds on a baking tray and roast for about 10 minutes until golden brown. Mix not too finely in the blender. Combine with the remaining spices.

Store the *dukkah* in a cool, dry place in a tightly closed jar.

MUSTARD SEEDS

At Boker Tov, we use mustard seeds to give dishes a fresh touch and greater depth. It goes perfectly with a sandwich, a salad or a vegetable dish.

INGREDIENTS

500 ml water
500 ml white wine vinegar
500 ml sushi vinegar
250 g yellow mustard seed

PREPARATION

Heat the water with the white wine vinegar, the sushi vinegar and the mustard seeds. Simmer over low heat for at least two hours until the mustard seeds have swollen and most of the moisture has evaporated. Leave to cool.

The mustard seeds will keep for at least a month in the refrigerator.

POMEGRANATE MOLASSES

FOR 180ML:
800 ml pomegranate juice
130 g sugar
70 ml fresh lemon juice

Boil the pomegranate juice with the sugar and lemon juice. Simmer over low heat for about 1 hour and 10 minutes. Stir every 10 minutes. Leave to cool completely.

The pomegranate molasses will keep for a month. You don't even have to put it in the fridge.

SILAN

Silan also goes under the name of date molasses or date honey. It's a very sweet syrup you can use as a sweetener in all kinds of dishes.

INGREDIENTS

PREPARATION

FOR 250ML:
650 g dates, pitted
1 l water

Place the dates in a bowl and cover with boiling water. Leave to soak for 10 minutes.

Remove the dates from the water. Boil a litre of clean water and add the soaked dates. Simmer for an hour and a half on low heat.

Let the dates cool completely in the cooking liquid. Place a straining cloth in a colander and place over a bowl. Pour the date mixture and drain completely. After that, reduce the sieved liquid to a thick syrup.

The syrup will keep in the refrigerator for at least three months.

HARISSA

3 red sweet pointed peppers
2 red chilli peppers
4 cloves of garlic
2 tbsp *biber salçası* (Turkish *labneh*pepper paste)
juice and zest of 1 lemon
1 tsp cumin powder
2 tsp smoked paprika powder
1 tsp red wine vinegar
1 tsp salt
65 ml olive oil

PREPARATION

Preheat the oven to 240°C.

Place the sweet peppers and chilli peppers on a baking tray and bake in the oven until they darken (you can also do this on the barbecue). Remove from the oven and leave to cool under a lid. Remove the skin and seeds from the sweet peppers. Peel the chilli peppers.

Place the sweet peppers and the chilli peppers in the blender with the peeled garlic, biber salçası, lemon juice and zest, cumin powder, paprika powder, red wine vinegar and salt. Add a drizzle of olive oil and mix to a smooth paste.

PRESERVED LEMONS

INGREDIENTS

10 organic lemons
coarse salt (preferably organic)
1 star anise pod
1 red chilli pepper

PREPARATION

Cut the lemons down to about 2 centimetres from the bottom. Fill with coarse salt. Push as many lemons as possible into a sterilized jar or preserving jar. Add the rest of the salt and star anise. Leave in the fridge for at least 3 weeks.

Cut the chilli pepper in half lengthwise and tuck it in with the lemon. Seal again and place in the fridge.

BASIC PREPARATIONS

BRINE FOR FRUITS AND VEGETABLES

For about 2 litres

We always have a few jars of pickled vegetables in our fridge. Pour the cold brine over various vegetables like small Persian cucumbers, shallots or cauliflower florets and serve them as side dishes in all kinds of preparations.

INGREDIENTS

1 red chilli pepper
1 l water
1 l natural vinegar
750 g cane sugar
5 g salt
5 star anise pods
5 fennel seeds
3 cardamom seeds

PREPARATION

Halve the chilli pepper. Heat the water and vinegar with the cane sugar, salt, star anise, fennel seeds, cardamom seeds and chilli pepper. Once the sugar has dissolved, remove from the heat and leave to cool.

CHICKEN BOUILLON

For about 6 litres

INGREDIENTS

1 (stewing) chicken
1 leek stalk
1 carrot
½ blanched celery
2 white onions
half a bulb of garlic
a handful of fresh thyme, rosemary and laurel leaves
1 tbsp peppercorns
1 star anise pod
1 tbsp salt
4 l water

PREPARATION

Preheat the oven to 180°C. Roast the chicken for 30 minutes.

Place the chicken in a cooking pot. Add the leek, carrot, celery, onions and garlic. Season with thyme, rosemary, laurel leaf, black peppercorns, star anise and salt. Add the water, bring to a boil and leave to simmer over a very low heat for about 8 hours, regularly skimming off fat and foam with a slotted spoon.

Strain the stock. Reduce a little for a stronger flavour.

YUZU VINAIGRETTE

We always have this vinaigrette at Boker Tov and at home to flavour salads, dishes and vegetables.

INGREDIENTS

300 ml sushi vinegar
300 ml olive oil
200 ml lemon juice
100 ml yuzu juice
1 tbsp sumac

PREPARATION

Mix the sushi vinegar with the oil, lemon juice, yuzu juice and sumac to form a vinaigrette.

The vinaigrette will keep for around a month in the refrigerator.

PICKLED GREEN PEPPERS

These pickled peppers are a side dish for about eight people.

INGREDIENTS

1 shallot
500 ml water
250 ml vinegar
2 tsp salt
1 laurel leaf
250 g green Turkish peppers

PREPARATION

Peel and chop the shallot. Boil the water with the shallot, vinegar, salt and laurel leaf.

Place the peppers in sterilized preserving jars or jars. Pour the boiling brine. Close the jars or preserving jars and place in a pot with gently boiling water for 5 minutes.

Leave the peppers to marinate for at least 24 hours. They will keep for three months in the refrigerator.

OLIVES

INGREDIENTS

½ tsp cumin seeds
½ tsp fennel seeds
1 blood orange
250 g high-quality green and black
olives
1 tbsp olive oil
1 laurel leaf
½ tsp dried oregano

PREPARATION

Toast the cumin seeds and fennel seeds in a non-stick pan without oil. Remove the peel and white pith from the orange and cut out the flesh segments (*peler à vif*).

Mix the olives with the olive oil, laurel leaf, oregano, roasted seeds and orange wedges.

LABNEH

Labneh is actually the Greek word for yoghurt, and it is often used in other languages too. If you let yoghurt drain for a long time, you get a creamy fresh cheese that is a must on any Middle Eastern table. Combine goat milk and cow milk yoghurt for an even better flavour.

INGREDIENTS

200 g goat milk yoghurt
300 g cow milk yoghurt
1 tsp salt

PREPARATION

Mix the yoghurt with the salt. Spoon everything into a sieve cloth and place in a colander. Leave to drain for at least 24 hours.

The *labneh* will keep for around five days in the refrigerator.

CHARIF

4 servings

Charif is a spicy tomato sauce for which you really need a very spicy jalapeño pepper.

INGREDIENTS

4 large tomatoes
1 jalapeño pepper
4 cloves of garlic
45 ml olive oil
3 tsp red wine vinegar
¼ tsp cumin powder
¼ tsp cayenne pepper
1 tsp salt
½ tsp sugar

PREPARATION

Cut the tomatoes into chunks. Remove the seeds and membranes from the pepper if you want a less spicy sauce. Peel the garlic.

Place the tomatoes with the pepper, garlic, olive oil, red wine vinegar, cumin powder, cayenne pepper, salt and sugar in a blender and blend for 3 minutes.

TAHINI

10 servings

At Boker Tov, we use *tahini* paste from Israel, Yemen or Lebanon, which has a finer flavour (less roasted) and is somewhat lighter in colour.

INGREDIENTS

5 cloves of garlic
170 ml fresh lemon juice
400 g *tahini* paste
2 tsp salt
1 tsp cumin powder
½ tsp black pepper
180 g cold water

PREPARATION

Peel the garlic and mix with the lemon juice for 2 minutes. Add the *tahini* paste, salt, cumin powder and pepper. Continue mixing. Drizzle in the water until the mixture has the consistency of mayonnaise.

This *tahini* will keep for at least a week in the refrigerator.

MISOTAHINI

10 servings

INGREDIENTS

5 cloves of garlic
170 ml fresh lemon juice
400 g *tahini* paste
1 tsp salt
1 tsp cumin powder
½ tsp black pepper
150 g cold water
30 ml ponzu (mirin-based sauce,
   found in Asian stores)
1 tbsp blonde miso (fermented
   soy beans, found in Asian stores)

PREPARATION

Peel the garlic and mix with the lemon juice for 2 minutes. Add the *tahini* paste, salt, cumin powder and pepper. Keep mixing. Add alternately ponzu, miso and a thin stream of water until the mixture has the consistency of mayonnaise.

This sauce will keep for at least a week in the refrigerator.

AMBA

10 servings

INGREDIENTS

1 ripe mango
2 cloves of garlic
juice of 2 limes
olive oil
1 tsp grain mustard
¼ tbsp fenugreek
¼ tbsp cayenne pepper
¼ tbsp smoked paprika powder
¼ tbsp salt
½ tbsp turmeric powder

PREPARATION

Peel the mango, remove the stone and cut the flesh into cubes. Mix finely in the blender. Peel the garlic and add the cloves to the mango. Add the lime juice, a dash of olive oil, grain mustard, fenugreek, cayenne pepper, paprika powder, salt and turmeric powder. Mix for 1 minute.

This sauce will keep for at least two weeks in the refrigerator.

GREEN ZHUG

Originally from Yemen, this spicy green sauce has since become a classic in Middle Eastern cuisine. You eat it, among other things, with falafel, grilled vegetables, fish, meat and eggs. It will keep for a few days in the fridge, but you can also freeze it in small portions so you always have some ready to use.

INGREDIENTS

3 red chilli peppers
6 cloves of garlic
1 bunch of coriander
1 bunch of flat-leaf parsley
1 bunch of dill
1 tbsp salt
1 tsp cumin powder
½ tsp coriander powder
500 ml olive oil
3 tbsp lemon juice

PREPARATION

Place the chilli peppers, peeled garlic cloves, coriander, flat-leaf parsley, dill, salt, cumin powder, coriander powder, olive oil and lemon juice in a blender. Blend to a smooth sauce.

You can keep green *zhug* for a while in the fridge or freezer.

RED ZHUG

Just like green *zhug* this sauce is also originally from Yemen. It is slightly spicier than the green version but gives your dishes the perfect boost. Make a generous amount and store in the fridge or in smaller portions in the freezer.

INGREDIENTS

20 red chilli peppers
6 cloves of garlic
½ bunch of coriander
1 tsp cumin powder
1 tbsp salt
400 ml olive oil
3 tbsp lemon juice

PREPARATION

Place the chilli peppers with the peeled garlic, coriander, cumin powder, salt, olive oil and lemon juice in a blender and blend until smooth.

You can keep red *zhug* for a while in the fridge or freezer.

HUMMUS

4 servings

Hummus is a basic ingredient in many dishes in the Middle East, North Africa and Turkey, but nowhere is it as smooth and creamy as in Israel. Use dried chickpeas that you soak for at least 24 hours and the best *tahini* paste.

INGREDIENTS

200 g dried chickpeas
1 tsp baking soda
2 cloves of garlic
10 g salt
4 g lemon pepper
30 g lemon juice
260 ml ice-cold water
1 tsp cumin seeds
275 g high-quality *tahini* paste
1 g citric acid

Scan me to find out more!

PREPARATION

Soak the chickpeas in plenty of cold water for 24 hours. Drain the water and cook the chickpeas in a large pot of water with baking soda for about 5 hours. Drain and leave to cool completely.

Mix 450 grams of cooked chickpeas with the peeled garlic, salt, lemon pepper, lemon juice, ice-cold water, cumin seeds, *tahini* and citric acid in a food processor to a smooth, fine paste.

BREAD

BAGELS

For 8 bagels

Originating from the Jewish communities in Poland as far back as 1600, bagels only became really popular when Jewish immigrants from Eastern Europe brought them to New York. Initially, they were only sold in the Jewish quarter, but they soon became popular everywhere. Vendors would drive around with carts full of bagels selling them all over town. In 1958, a machine was invented that simplified their production. Meanwhile, you can also get them here at any supermarket, but they are even tastier when you make them yourself.

INGREDIENTS

275 ml water
15 g fresh yeast
500 g flour
15 g honey

10 g sunflower oil
5 g sugar
15 g salt

PREPARATION

Slightly heat 100 millilitres of water and dissolve the fresh yeast in it. Place the flour in the food processor bowl with the rest of the water, honey, sunflower oil and sugar. Sprinkle salt on top. Add the water and yeast. With the kneading hook, knead for about 8 minutes to a homogeneous dough.

Form balls of about 100 grams each and leave to rest for 15 minutes. Punch a hole in the centre of each ball with your finger and knead them smoothly into bagel shapes. Leave the bagels to rise for an hour.

Preheat the oven to 200°C.

Cook the bagels for 2 minutes in lightly boiling water. Turn them over and let them cook for another 2 minutes. Line a baking tray with baking paper. Remove the bagels from the water with a slotted spoon, drain briefly and place on the baking tray.

Finish the bagels with black or white sesame seeds or poppy seeds. Bake in the oven for about 15 minutes until golden brown. Place on a wire rack to cool.

CHALLAH

For 2 loaves

Challah is a typical Jewish braided bread traditionally served on Friday evenings before the *shabbat* is eaten. It is sweet and resembles a brioche. The braiding takes some skill, but the final result looks very nice.

INGREDIENTS

340 g water
55 g fresh yeast
125 g honey
4 eggs

975 g flour
18 g salt
140 g butter at room temperature
white sesame seeds

PREPARATION

Preheat the oven at 180 °C.

Heat the water and dissolve the yeast in it. Place in the food processor bowl with the honey, eggs, flour and salt. Knead with the food processor K blade. Add the butter in small cubes.

Leave to cool and divide in four. Divide each piece again in four. Roll out each piece separately to an approximately 30-centimetre sausage. Braid them into two beautiful *challahs*.

Line a baking tray with baking paper. Place the *challahs* on the baking sheet and leave them to rise at room temperature for at least an hour until they double in size. Sprinkle generously with white sesame seeds. Bake for 25 minutes in the preheated oven until golden brown.

Place on a wire rack to cool.

ZA'ATAR FLATBREAD

For 4 flatbreads

Flatbread is a very ancient way of making bread, originating from ancient Egypt. The bread is often baked in a brick oven, but at home it can also be baked in a regular oven. In the Middle East, flatbread is served with many savoury dishes.

INGREDIENTS

295 g water
1 tsp dry yeast
2 tsp (organic) salt
1 tbsp granulated sugar

420 g 00 flour
1 tbsp canola oil
120 ml olive oil
120 g za'atar (recipe p. 36)

PREPARATION

Preheat the oven to 180°C.

Heat the water to around 45°C and mix with the yeast, salt and sugar. Mix in the flour with your hands. Add the canola oil and knead into a firm dough.

Divide the dough into four equal pieces and roll out each piece with a rolling pin. Mix the olive oil with the za'atar. Brush the flatbreads generously with this.

Line a baking tray with baking paper. Bake the breads for 20 minutes in the oven.

TIP: If possible, bake the breads in a pizza oven. Then they're even tastier.

LAFFA

For 10 pieces of *laffa*

Laffa is a type of flatbread, also sometimes known as Iraqi pita. You can't cut this bread open like a pita; instead, you dip it or roll something in it.

INGREDIENTS

900 g 00 flour
7 g dry yeast
2 tbsp granulated sugar

1 tsp salt
4 tbsp olive oil
720 g water

PREPARATION

Mix the flour, yeast, granulated sugar and salt in the food processor. Slowly add the oil and water. Knead with a dough hook to an elastic dough.

Cover with cling foil and a kitchen towel. Leave to rise for about an hour in a warm place.

Knead the dough again thoroughly when it has doubled in volume. Divide into ten equal parts. Shape into balls and cover with a damp kitchen towel. Leave to rise for another 15 minutes.

Heat a grill pan or frying pan on the stove. Flatten the balls with a rolling pin and fry them in the hot pan for about 1 minute on each side.

You can store these breads in the freezer so you always have some at hand.

BREAKFAST

SHAKSHUKA

4 servings

The *shakshuka* sauce needs to be cooked for a few hours to get a warm, full structure.
If you're not an early riser, it's better to prepare it the day before.

INGREDIENTS

4 eggs
2 white onions
6 cloves of garlic
100 ml sunflower oil
2 tsp *harissa*
1 tbsp *ras el hanout*
2 tbsp smoked paprika powder
salt

black pepper
1 kg tomatoes
2 tbsp mild *biber salçası*
(Turkish pepper paste)
2 yellow bell peppers
2 red bell peppers
2 red chilli peppers

PREPARATION

Chop the onions and grate the garlic. Sauté them in the oil in a deep pan that is
suitable to be used in the oven. Season with the *harissa, ras el hanout*, paprika powder,
salt and pepper. Leave to cook together for one minute. Quarter the tomatoes and add
to the mixture along with the *biber salçası*. Simmer for one hour on a low heat.

Preheat the oven to 240°C. Place the bell peppers and chilli peppers on a baking tray
and bake in the oven until the skin darkens (you can also do this on the barbecue).
Remove from the oven and leave to cool under a lid. Peel the bell peppers and remove
the seeds and membranes. Cut the flesh into chunks and add to the tomato sauce.
Simmer for one hour over low heat until the sauce has thickened and is full of flavour.

Make wells in the sauce. Break an egg into each well and place the pan in the oven for
about 10 minutes (or until the egg whites set).

Serve the *shakshuka* with flatbread (p. 62), *tahini* (p. 47), green herbs and pickled
vegetables.

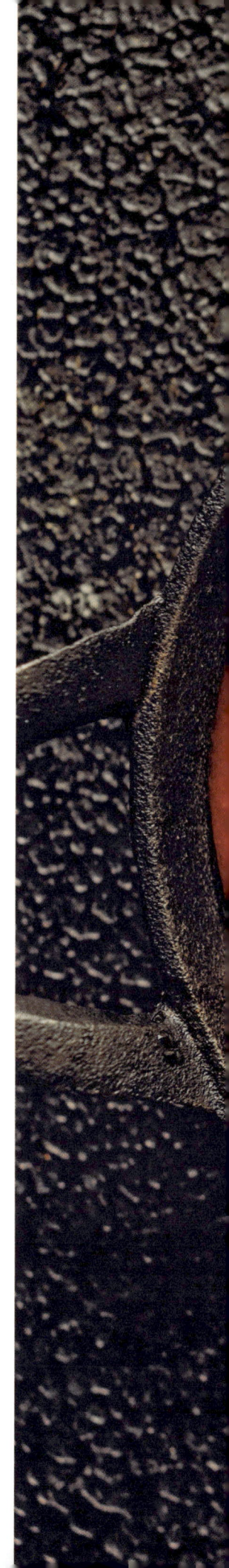

ZA'ATAR EGGS

1 serving

INGREDIENTS

1 tsp baking soda
olive oil
3 eggs
¼ tsp *za'atar*

black pepper
salt
a few sprigs of flat-leaf parsley

PREPARATION

Melt the butter in a pan with the olive oil.

Break in the eggs and fry over a medium heat. Season with *za'atar*, black pepper and salt. Garnish with chopped flat-leaf parsley.

FUL

4 servings

INGREDIENTS

2 cans cooked broad beans
  (*fava beans*, 400 g per can)
120 ml water
1 red chilli pepper
2 cloves of garlic
1 tsp cumin powder

1 tomato cut into chunks
3 tbsp olive oil
juice and zest of 1 lemon
5 g flat-leaf parsley
1 tsp salt
black pepper

PREPARATION

Drain the beans and rinse under running water. Place in a cooking pot with the water and bring to a boil to warm them up. Drain the beans again and crush with a fork.

Crush the chilli pepper with the peeled garlic and the cumin powder in a mortar. Add the paste to the beans.

Mix the tomato, olive oil, lemon juice, lemon zest and chopped flat-leaf parsley with the beans. Season with salt and black pepper.

GRANOLA

INGREDIENTS

150 g pecans	200 g oat flakes
50 g coconut butter	100 g almond shavings
125 g honey	4 g cardamom powder
125 g maple syrup	zest of 1 orange

PREPARATION

Preheat the oven to 160°C.

Course chop the pecans. Melt the coconut butter and mix with the honey, maple syrup, chopped pecans, oat flakes, almonds and cardamom powder.

Line a baking tray with baking paper. Distribute the mixture on the baking tray and bake for 10 minutes in the oven. Mix and bake for another 10 minutes. The granola needs to be thoroughly dry.

Remove the granola from the oven and mix with the orange zest.

FRENCH TOAST

1 serving

Pain perdu, but then the Middle Eastern way with pomegranate molasses, cream and almonds. Not a breakfast for the faint-hearted! Preferably use *challah* that you can find at the Jewish bakery, or bake it yourself.

INGREDIENTS

3 eggs
500 ml whole milk
15 g powdered sugar
1 g cinnamon powder
1 g cardamom powder
20 g butter

2 slices of *challah*, 2 cm thick (recipe p.58)
2 tbsp pomegranate molasses (recipe p. 40)
15 g almond shavings
½ pomegranate
50 g crème fraîche
zest of 1 orange

PREPARATION

Beat the eggs with the milk, powdered sugar, cinnamon powder and cardamom powder.

Melt the butter in a frying pan. Dip the bread in the egg mixture and allow it to drain a little. Fry it in the pan until golden brown on both sides. Brush the top of each slice of bread with pomegranate molasses.

Toast the almond shavings in a non-stick pan without oil. Remove the seeds from the pomegranate. Spread the crème fraiche on the bread and sprinkle the toasted almonds and pomegranate seeds over the bread. Finish with some orange zest.

BOREKAS

4 servings

In Israel, *borekas* are a common breakfast snack. You can buy them at any grocery store or supermarket, but it's actually not that difficult to make them yourself. Of course, you can also eat these *borekas* for lunch.

INGREDIENTS

500 g assortment of mushrooms (oyster mushrooms, portobello, shiitake...)
200 g pickled silver onions
25 g butter
3 g lemon pepper
2 g sumac
2 g *za'atar* (recipe p. 36)
3 g *pul biber* (flakes from Aleppo pepper)

black pepper
salt
50 g baby spinach
150 g goat cheese
juice and zest of 1 lemon
1 sheet or 4 squares of puff pastry
1 egg yolk
1 tsp sesame seeds

PREPARATION

Preheat the oven to 180°C.

Wash the mushrooms. Drain the silver onions. Fry the mushrooms with the silver onions in the butter. Season with lemon pepper, sumac, *za'atar*, chilli flakes, freshly ground pepper and salt.

Add the spinach and cook for 1 minute. Remove from the heat and crumble in the goat cheese. Stir well. Mix the lemon juice and zest with the mushrooms and spinach.

Cut the puff pastry into approximately 12 x 12-centimetre squares. Place a heaping tablespoon of the mixture in the centre.

Beat the egg yolk. Brush the edges of the puff pastry with egg yolk and fold into a triangle. Seal the edges with a fork and brush the top with egg yolk. Sprinkle some sesame seeds over it.

Line a baking tray with baking paper. Place the *borekas* on the baking tray and bake for 15 minutes in the oven.

TEL AVIV CROQUE MADAME

4 servings

A croque madame as it is served in Tel Aviv with feta and pastrami and finished with *za'atar* eggs. Bet you'll never want a regular croque madame again once you've tasted this one!

INGREDIENTS

8 thin slices of *challah* (recipe p. 58)
250 g feta
400 g pastrami (sliced)
20 g red *zhug* (recipe p. 51)

50 g butter
25 g olive oil
4 *za'atar* eggs (recipe p. 68)

PREPARATION

Crumble half of the feta over four slices of *challah*. Place the pastrami on top and crumble the rest of the feta over it.

Spread red *zhug* on the four remaining slices and place these on the slices with the feta and pastrami.

Melt the butter in a frying pan with the olive oil. Fry the toasts until golden brown on both sides. Fry *za'atar* eggs in another pan. Place the eggs on the croque madame.

Serve with pickled cucumbers, *Fattoush salad* (p. 88) and *tahini* (p. 47).

PICKLED SALMON

4 servings

INGREDIENTS

750 ml white wine (not too expensive!)
200 ml Noilly Prat
45 ml arrack (strong alcoholic beverage)
80 g salt
95 g sugar

1 tbsp peppercorns
1 salmon fillet with skin, +/- 500 g
fennel trimmings
parsley stems

PREPARATION

Boil the white wine with the Noilly Prat, arrack, salt, sugar and peppercorns. Once the sugar has dissolved, remove from the heat and leave to cool completely.

Place the salmon in a large container. Pour the mixture over it. Add fennel and parsley stems, if desired.

Cover and leave in the refrigerator for 12 hours. Turn the salmon over and allow to marinate for another 12 hours.

Rinse the salmon under ice-cold water. Remove the skin and cut into 5-millimetre slices.

POACHED EGGS WITH LABNEH AND ALEPPO PEPPER BUTTER

4 servings

Pul biber, made from Aleppo peppers, has a nice and fruity flavour that slightly resembles cumin. The peppers are dried and ground into flakes and used in many dishes. You can sprinkle them over meat or make a spicy butter out of them, like we do here.

INGREDIENTS

75 g salted butter
1 tbsp *pul biber* (flakes from Aleppo pepper)
1 clove of grated garlic
1 tsp salt
1 tbsp natural vinegar
4 eggs

400 g *Labneh* (recipe p. 46)
160 g pickled cauliflower (recipe for brine p. 44)
a few sprigs of fresh dill
coarse sea salt

PREPARATION

Melt the butter with the *pul biber*. Add the garlic and the salt. Leave to simmer.

Boil water in a saucepan with the vinegar. Stir with a whisk, creating a whirlpool. Break the eggs one at a time into a cup and slide gently into the water. Cook for 2 minutes.

Distribute some *labneh* over a plate. Place the poached eggs and pickled cauliflower on top.

Garnish with the chilli butter, dill and coarse sea salt.

TO SHARE

BALAGAN

As mentioned before, the Balagan Box is a very important part of Boker Tov. Balagan means 'cozy mess' in Hebrew, but in this case it refers to a collection of tasty snacks. With the Balagan Box, you can make a delicious meal in no less than 15 minutes. All you need is an oven.

It's easy, fun, cozy, ideal for small and bigger groups and the perfect introduction to the Israeli kitchen.

FATTOUSH SALAD

4 servings

Fattoush is a typical Middle Eastern salad with pieces of dried pita or Lebanese bread. You garnish it with sumac, which is made from grounded red berries, giving the dish a fresh touch.

INGREDIENTS

4 small Persian cucumbers
100 g cherry tomatoes
1 bunch of radishes
1 red onion
3 spring onions
1 pomegranate
handful of chopped green herbs (parsley, dill, coriander, mint)
1 tsp coarse sea salt

1 g white pepper
50 g buttermilk
50 g olive oil
30 g lemon juice
20 g white wine vinegar
5 g sumac
1 clove of grated garlic
2 loaves of Lebanese bread or pita breads

PREPARATION

Dice the cucumbers and halve the cherry tomatoes. Wash and dice the radishes. Peel the onions and cut them into thin strips. Course chop the spring onions. Beat the seeds out of the pomegranate with a wooden spoon. Mix everything together and add the chopped herbs. Season with sea salt and freshly ground pepper.

Mix the buttermilk with the olive oil, lemon juice, vinegar and sumac to form a vinaigrette. Add the grated garlic.

Cut the Lebanese bread or pita breads into pieces and toast them in the oven at 160°C. Break into smaller pieces. Mix the crackers through the salad.

TABBOULEH

4 servings

INGREDIENTS

75 g bulgur
4 bunches of fresh parsley
2 bunches of mint
1 bunch of spring onions
100 g cherry tomatoes
4 small Persian cucumbers

5 g lemon pepper
10 g cumin powder
juice of 2 lemons
75 ml olive oil
black pepper
salt

PREPARATION

Cook the bulgur as indicated on the package. Leave to cool completely.

Fine chop the parsley, mint, spring onions, cherry tomatoes and cucumbers and mix them with the cooked bulgur. Stir in the lemon pepper, cumin powder, lemon juice and olive oil. Season with pepper and salt.

BARBECUED AUBERGINES

4 servings

INGREDIENTS

4 aubergines
100 g cherry tomatoes
10 g ponzu sauce
25 g chilli garlic sauce

120 g *tahini* (recipe p. 47)
80 g green *zhug* (recipe p. 51)
olive oil
fleur de sel

PREPARATION

Preheat the barbecue (or the oven to 180°C). Roast the aubergines for about 20 minutes (27 minutes in the oven) until fully cooked.

Score the aubergines under the green stem all the way around and carefully remove the skin without breaking the flesh.

Mix the cherry tomatoes with the ponzu sauce for 1 minute and then sieve the mixture. Stir in the chilli garlic sauce to create a nice spicy mixture.

Halve the aubergines lengthwise and roast them briefly on the barbecue until they're hot. Place half an aubergine on a plate. Add *tahini*, green *zhug* and the tomato mixture. Garnish with pepper and *fleur de sel*.

SEABASS CEVICHE WITH SUMAC AND PUL BIBER

4 servings

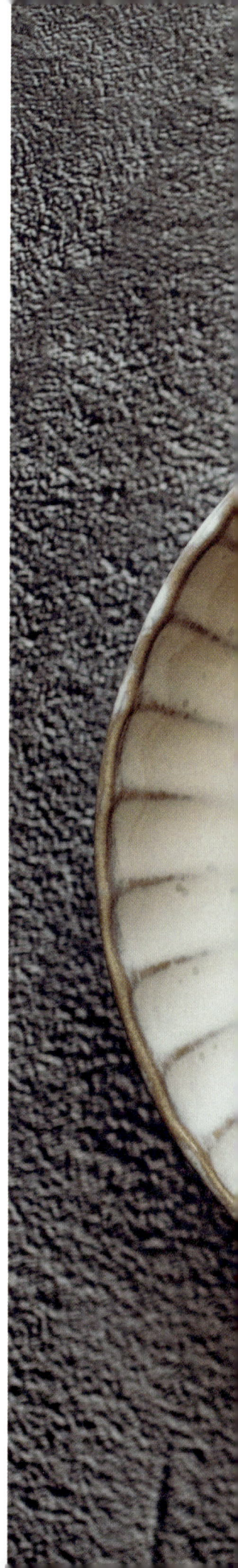

INGREDIENTS

500 g skinless sea bass fillet
1 red onion
1 red chilli pepper
1 sour apple (e.g., Granny Smith)
2 small Persian cucumbers
1 ripe avocado
2 limes
fish sauce
fleur de sel
olive oil
½ a bunch of coriander
12 g sumac
200 ml *leche de tigre*

FOR THE LECHE DE TIGRE

4 shallots
4 cloves of garlic
100 g fresh ginger
5 stems of lemongrass
1 l strong vegetable bouillon
100 ml sushi vinegar
100 ml lemon juice
100 ml high-quality fish sauce
5 kaffir lime leaves
handful of mint and coriander
1 tbsp *pul biber* (flakes from Aleppo pepper)

PREPARATION

First make the *leche de tigre*. Cut the shallots coarsely. Grate the garlic and the ginger. Crush the lemongrass and finely chop the inside. Place the shallots, garlic, ginger, lemongrass, bouillon, vinegar, lemon juice, fish sauce, kaffir lime leaves, mint, coriander and *pul biber* in a large bowl and mix briefly. Leave for at least 4 hours to infuse. Pour through a fine sieve. The flavour should be salty and spicy. Add extra lemon juice, soy sauce or chilli pepper according to taste. Leave to cool completely in the refrigerator.

Cut the sea bass into very thin slices. Peel the onion and cut into thin strips. Cut the chilli pepper into fine strips and the apple, cucumber and avocado into chunks. Juice the limes.

Place the sea bass slices in a bowl. Marinate briefly in the lime juice, fish sauce, olive oil and *fleur de sel*. Mix the apple chunks with the cucumber and avocado. Spoon some of the mixture over the sea bass. Add some red onion and a few sprigs of coriander. Garnish with the ice-cold *leche de tigre*.

YOU
THE CH
TO
HUM

'RE
ICKPEA
MY
MUS

AUTUMN HUMMUS WITH STEWED MUSHROOMS

4 servings

INGREDIENTS

400 g mushrooms (a mix of oyster
   mushrooms, portobello, penny buns,
   chanterelles, etc.)
2 red onions
50 g butter
2 cloves of grated garlic
black pepper

salt
½ a bunch of flat-leaf parsley
1 tbsp smoked paprika powder
400 g hummus (recipe p. 52)
olive oil

PREPARATION

Wash the mushrooms and cut the red onions into fine strips. Fry the mushrooms in the butter. Add the onion and grated garlic. Season with pepper and salt. Coarse chop the parsley and mix with the mushrooms. Finish with smoked paprika.

Scoop the hummus onto the plates. Place the mushrooms on top and finish with a drizzle of olive oil.

WINTER HUMMUS WITH BARBECUE VEGETABLES

4 servings

INGREDIENTS

1 aubergine
2 small Persian cucumbers
2 spring onions
60 g cherry tomatoes
30 g black olives
handful of green herbs (dill, coriander, flat-leaf parsley)

juice and zest of 1 lemon
1 tsp cumin powder
black pepper
salt
400 g hummus (recipe p.52)
olive oil

PREPARATION

Heat the barbecue. Roast the aubergine for about 20 minutes.

Cut the cucumbers into thick strips and the spring onions into slices of 3 centimetres. Grill the cucumbers, tomatoes and spring onions on the barbecue.

Scrape the flesh from the aubergine and mix with the roasted vegetables. Stir in the coarsely chopped herbs, lemon juice and zest. Season with cumin powder, pepper and salt.

Scoop the hummus onto the plates. Place the roasted vegetables on top and finish with olive oil.

SPRING HUMMUS WITH MINCED MEAT AND PINE NUTS

4 servings

INGREDIENTS

30 g pine nuts
olive oil
100 g minced lamb
100 g minced beef
2 cloves of grated garlic
black pepper

salt
80 g cherry tomatoes
1 tsp allspice
400 g hummus (recipe p. 52)
1/3 bunch of fresh parsley

PREPARATION

Fry the pine nuts in olive oil until golden brown.

Fry the minced meat in olive oil and add the grated garlic. Season with pepper and salt. Halve the cherry tomatoes and add to the minced meat with the allspice. Leave to cook for another minute and remove from the heat.

Scoop the hummus onto the plates. Top with the minced meat and finish with coarsely chopped flat-leaf parsley, the toasted pine nuts and some extra olive oil.

SUMMER HUMMUS WITH EGG AND TOMATO SALAD

4 servings

INGREDIENTS

2 eggs
a dash of natural vinegar
400 g hummus (recipe p. 52)
120 g cherry tomatoes
olive oil

juice of 1 lemon
black pepper
salt
½ a bunch of flat-leaf parsley

PREPARATION

Put the eggs in a saucepan with water and a dash of vinegar. Boil the water for 5 minutes. Place the hard-boiled eggs in ice-cold water and peel them. Cut the eggs in half.

Halve the cherry tomatoes and toss with olive oil and lemon juice. Season with pepper and salt. Scoop the hummus onto the plates and place cherry tomatoes and half an egg on each plate.

Garnish with coarsely chopped flat-leaf parsley and a drizzle of olive oil.

TA'AMEYA (EGYPTIAN FALAFEL)

4 servings

INGREDIENTS

500 g dry broad beans
1 bunch of coriander
1 bunch of fresh flat-leaf parsley
½ bunch of dill
½ bunch of spring onions
3 cloves of garlic

2 tbsp cumin powder
½ tsp baking powder
1 g white pepper
1 tsp salt
frying oil

PREPARATION

Soak the broad beans for 24 hours in cold water. Drain the water out through a sieve.

Coarse chop the coriander, parsley, dill and spring onions. Mix the soaked broad beans with the herbs, garlic, cumin powder, baking powder, white pepper and salt in a food processor until you get a homogeneous paste.

Make falafel balls (preferably use a falafel scoop).

Heat the frying oil to 180°C and fry the falafels for 4 minutes. Place on kitchen paper to absorb excess oil and sprinkle with some salt.

BOKER TOV CHICKEN SCHNITZEL

4 servings

INGREDIENTS

1 kg chicken thighs with bones removed
2 g *pul biber* (flakes from Aleppo pepper)
5 g cumin powder
5 g turmeric powder
2 g cinnamon powder
4 g *ras el hanout* (recipe p. 36)
9 g mild paprika powder
5 g salt
4 cloves of grated garlic

30 ml lemon juice
40 ml olive oil
2 g white pepper
flour
2 eggs
bread crumbs
cornflakes
sunflower oil

PREPARATION

Place the chicken meat between two sheets of baking paper and hit with a pan to flatten it. Rub in the *pul biber*, cumin powder, turmeric powder, cinnamon powder, *ras el hanout*, paprika powder, salt, grated garlic, lemon juice, olive oil and pepper. Leave to marinate for 1 hour.

Place the flour in a bowl. Beat the eggs in a second bowl. Mix the bread crumbs with the cornflakes in a 70/30 ratio.

First roll the chicken in the flour. Then dip in the eggs and finally in the bread crumbs/ cornflakes mix.

Sauté the chicken in sunflower oil for 2 minutes on each side until golden brown.

CHIC
SCHN
IN PAR

KEN

TZEL

ADISE

COLESLAW

4 servings

INGREDIENTS

100 g grated carrots	salt
100 g grated white cabbage	juice of 1 lemon
100 g grated red cabbage	50 ml olive oil
black pepper	

PREPARATION

Mix the carrots with the white and red cabbage. Season with pepper and salt. Stir in the lemon juice and olive oil.

ROASTED CARROTS WITH CHERMOULA AND HARISSA

4 servings

INGREDIENTS

juice and zest of 1 lemon
4 tbsp *chermoula* mayonnaise (recipe p. 127)
2 tbsp *harissa* (recipe p. 41)
1 cup fresh chervil

2 bunches of baby carrots
1 tbsp honey
1 tsp maple syrup
2 tbsp olive oil

1 tbsp smoked paprika powder
1 clove of grated garlic
black pepper
salt
5 g sumac

PREPARATION

Preheat the oven to 180°C.

Wash the carrots. Cut off the carrot tops, leaving about 4 centimetres.

Mix the honey with the maple syrup, olive oil, *pul biber*, smoked paprika powder and grated garlic. Season with pepper and salt. Toss the carrots in the marinade. Place on a baking tray lined with baking paper and bake them for 25 minutes in the oven.

Remove the carrots from the oven and finish with sumac, lemon juice and zest. Add *chermoula* mayonnaise, *harissa* and tufts of fresh chervil.

COURGETTE AND BURRATA SALAD

4 servings

INGREDIENTS

1 baby fennel
1 yellow courgette
1 green courgette
20 g olive oil
3 cloves of grated garlic
30 g smoked olive oil
30 g lemon juice
10 g sumac

black pepper
salt
2 burrata cheeses
100 g samphire
1 red onion
1 g *pul biber* (flakes from Aleppo pepper)
wild, edible flowers from the garden

PREPARATION

Cut the fennel into wafer-thin slices on the mandolin. Place in ice-cold water with ice cubes for an hour.

Also cut the yellow and green courgettes into wafer-thin slices. Remove the fennel from the water, pat dry and mix with the courgette slices.

Heat the olive oil in a small pan. Add the grated garlic and sauté for 2 minutes on a low heat until golden (not brown). Remove the pan from the heat and add the smoked olive oil and lemon juice. Season with sumac, pepper and salt.

Pour the dressing over the courgettes and fennel. Season with pepper and salt to taste.

Place the vegetables in a bowl. Cut open the burrata cheese and place the balls on the salad. Drizzle some olive oil over it and sprinkle with *pul biber*. Finish with wild, edible flowers— preferably flowers with an aniseed or basil flavour.

Serve with freshly baked *laffa* bread (recipe p.63).

CELERIAC

CELERIAC WITH GOAT CHEESE AND GRILLED GRAPES

4 servings

INGREDIENTS

½ celery root
200 g blue grapes
4 sprigs of thyme
1 Jonagold apple
80 g peeled hazelnuts
200 g hard goat cheese

1 tbsp honey
juice of 2 lemons
1 tsp *pul biber* (flakes from Aleppo pepper)
black pepper
salt

PREPARATION

Peel and grate the celery root.

Grill the grapes on the barbecue or in a grill pan. Remove the thyme from the stem. Slice the apple into thin strips and coarse chop the hazelnuts. Crumble the goat cheese.

Gently mix the grapes, thyme, apple, hazelnuts and goat cheese with the celery root. Add the honey and the lemon juice. Season with *pul biber*, pepper and salt.

PTITIM ISRAELI COUSCOUS

4 servings

INGREDIENTS

300 g hand-rolled couscous
3 Persian cucumbers
400 g cherry tomatoes
1 red onion
1 bunch of spring onions
1 bunch of radishes
handful of green herbs (mint, coriander, flat-leaf parsley, dill)

4 tbsp olive oil
juice of 2 lemons
1 tsp sumac
1 tsp za'atar (recipe p. 36)
black pepper
salt
400 g fresh cherries
1 pomegranate

PREPARATION

Prepare the couscous as stated on the package. Cool to room temperature.

Dice the cucumbers, cherry tomatoes, onion, spring onions and radishes. Mix the vegetables with the couscous. Coarse chop the green herbs and mix into the salad. Add the olive oil and lemon juice to the salad. Season with sumac, za'atar, pepper and salt.

Pit and halve the cherries. Remove the seeds from the pomegranate. Gently mix into the salad.

BIG BITES

CHICKEN SCHNITZEL & COLESLAW IN LEBANESE BREAD

4 servings

INGREDIENTS

1 pack of Lebanese bread (4 pieces)
300 g coleslaw (recipe p. 110)
120 g *Fattoush* salad (recipe p. 88)
4 chicken schnitzels (recipe p. 106)

24 g red *zhug* (recipe p. 51)
80 g *tahini* (recipe p. 47)
handful of green herbs (mint, dill, coriander, flat-leaf parsley)

PREPARATION

Cut open the bread and line with coleslaw. Add the *Fattoush* salad. Cut the fried chicken schnitzel into three and place on top of the salad. Finish with red *zhug*, *tahini* and coarsely chopped green herbs.

Carefully roll up the bread and bake for 2 minutes between two grill plates (like a panini).

PASTRAMI SANDWICH

4 servings

INGREDIENTS

8 slices of *challah*, 1 centimetre thick (recipe p. 58)
120 g *tahini* (recipe p. 47)
450 g coleslaw (recipe p. 110)
500 g pastrami

handful of green herbs (mint, dill, coriander, flat-leaf parsley)
4 pickled cucumbers (recipe p. 44)
4 g *za'atar*

PREPARATION

Toast the bread. Spread half the *tahini* on the toasted bread. Add half of the coleslaw on top. Top with the pastrami and add the remaining coleslaw and *tahini*.

Coarse chop the green herbs and add these with the pickled cucumber to the sandwich.

Finish with some *za'atar* and place the second slice of toast on top.

SABICH

4 servings

Sabich is also known as a Tel Aviv sandwich and is by far our favourite sandwich. It is a pita bread filled with roasted aubergines and a few spicy sauces..

INGREDIENTS

2 aubergines
salt
black pepper
4 tbsp olive oil
1 clove of garlic
4 pita breads

200 g hummus (recipe p. 52)
80 g *amba* (recipe p. 50)
40 g red *zhug* (recipe p. 51)
4 hard-boiled eggs
200 g *Fattoush* salad (recipe p. 88)

PREPARATION

Cut the aubergines into 1-centimetre-thick slices and roast in a grill pan. Mix the olive oil with the grated garlic and season with salt and pepper. Place the grilled aubergines in the oil.

Grill the pita breads for 2 minutes in the oven. Cut off the tops and spread hummus, *amba* and red *zhug* inside.

Slice the eggs.

Fill the breads with the roasted aubergine, eggs and *Fattoush* salad.

TIP: Serve with extra *tahini* to taste.

FLOWER POWER CAULIFLOWER

4 servings

INGREDIENTS

1 cauliflower
1 tbsp turmeric powder
black pepper
salt
150 g butter
1 orange zest
fleur de sel
70 g *chermoula* mayonnaise
70 g *harissa* (recipe p. 41)
70 g *tahini* (recipe p. 47)

FOR THE CHERMOULA MAYONNAISE

½ a bunch of flat-leaf parsley
½ a bunch of coriander
2 cloves of garlic
1 tsp *pul biber* (flakes from Aleppo pepper)
15 ml olive oil
1 tbsp white wine vinegar
1 tsp mustard
juice of 1 lemon
salt
black pepper
500 g mayonnaise

PREPARATION

First make the *chermoula* mayonnaise. Mix the flat-leaf parsley with the coriander, garlic, *pul biber*, olive oil, white wine vinegar, mustard and lemon juice. Season with pepper and salt. Add the mayonnaise and mix for a few minutes.

Cut the cauliflower into 2-centimetre-thick slices. Season with turmeric, pepper and salt. Melt the butter and fry the slices for about 10 minutes on each side. Garnish with lemon zest and *fleur de sel*.

Place the cauliflower on a plate and serve with *chermoula* mayonnaise, *harissa* and *tahini*.

YOU'
FCK
AWE

TASTE
ING
SOME

TELADOG

4 servings

You won't find hot dogs in Israel, because they usually contain pork. But for Tom, a tasty hot dog was a must in the restaurant—sort of an ode to the pop-up sausage stand he used to own. So he came up with a Middle Eastern version with merguez sausages, *harissa* ketchup and *tahini*, or as he calls it, a teladog. In Tom's words, the perfect bridge between Tel Aviv and Antwerp.

INGREDIENTS

50 g ketchup
50 g *harissa* (recipe p. 41)
4 merguez sausages
4 hot dog buns with sesame seeds

80 g *tahini* (recipe p. 47)
90 g coleslaw (recipe p. 110)
4 pickled cucumbers (recipe p. 44)
40 g *dukkah* (recipe p. 37)

PREPARATION

Mix the ketchup and the *harissa*. Grill the sausages in a grill pan.

Cut open the buns and toast briefly in the oven. Fill each bun with *harissa*, ketchup, *tahini*, coleslaw, a sausage, pickled cucumber and *dukkah*.

CHRAIME WITH COURGETTES

4 servings

Chraime is a thick, spicy tomato sauce that is often served with fish in the Middle East, but in this version, we have replaced the fish with minced lamb and stuffed courgette balls.

INGREDIENTS

150 g brown rice
1 onion
2 cloves of garlic
1 red chilli pepper
30 ml olive oil
150 g minced lamb
1 tsp cumin powder
½ tsp *pul biber* (flakes from Aleppo pepper)
1 tsp coriander powder
1 tsp turmeric powder
650 ml chicken bouillon

1 can (400 g) chickpeas
50 g peas (frozen)
juice of 1 lemon
1 bunch of parsley
1 bunch of coriander
150 g feta
4 round courgettes (or regular courgettes)
black pepper
salt

FOR THE CHRAIME

8 tsp sunflower oil
5 cloves of garlic
1 tsp caraway seeds
1 tsp *pul biber* (flakes from Aleppo pepper)
2 tbsp paprika powder
1 tbsp cumin powder
3 tbsp tomato purée (concentrated)
water
juice of 1 lemon
1 tbsp cane sugar
cinnamon powder
black pepper
salt

PREPARATION

First make the *chraime*. Heat the oil in a pan. Add the grated garlic, caraway seeds, *pul biber*, paprika and cumin. Add the tomato purée and cook together for a while. Deglaze with a little water. Leave to simmer for a few minutes and add the lemon juice and cane sugar. Season with a pinch of cinnamon powder, pepper and salt. Leave to simmer for around 10 minutes. It's normal for the oil to separate from the sauce.

Preheat the oven to 180°C.

Place the rice in a sieve and rinse under cold running water.

Chop the onion, garlic and chilli pepper and fry them in the olive oil. Add the minced lamb and fry as well. Season with the cumin powder, *pul biber*, coriander and turmeric. Stir the rice into the meat. Deglaze with the bouillon. Simmer over low heat until the rice is cooked.

Drain the chickpeas. Add them to the rice along with the lemon juice, chopped parsley and coriander. Crumble in the feta.

Halve the courgettes and hollow out with a spoon. Brush the insides with some extra olive oil and grill briefly in a hot pan. Season the insides with pepper and salt. Fill with the rice mixture.

Place the courgettes on an oven tray and bake for 20 minutes in the oven.

Serve the courgettes with the *chraime* sauce and garnish with fresh coriander.

BARBECUED SEA BREAM WITH MANY SIDE DISHES

4 servings

You prepare this bream on the barbecue and serve it with many side dishes, the recipes for these side dishes are included elsewhere in this book.

INGREDIENTS

2 red chilli peppers
4 cloves of garlic
50 g thyme
olive oil
black pepper
salt
2 sea breams, about 850 g each, washed but not filleted
2 lemons

FOR THE SIDE DISHES

tahini (recipe p. 47)
green *zhug* (recipe p. 51)
tabbouleh (recipe p. 90) with grapefruit
Fattoush salad (recipe p. 88)
pickled vegetables (recipe p. 44)
za'atar bread (recipe p. 62)

PREPARATION

Remove the seeds from the chillies and cut into thin rings. Press the garlic. Remove the thyme leaves. Mix the chilli, garlic and thyme with 4 tablespoons of olive oil. Season with pepper and salt.

Wash the fish and pat dry. Score the skin a few times with a sharp knife. Rub the fish inside and outside with the herb oil. Season with pepper and salt. Roast on the hot barbecue for 5 to 7 minutes until golden brown and crispy.

Halve the lemons and place it face down on the barbecue, until they turn a dark colour.

Serve the bream with the lemons and all the side dishes.

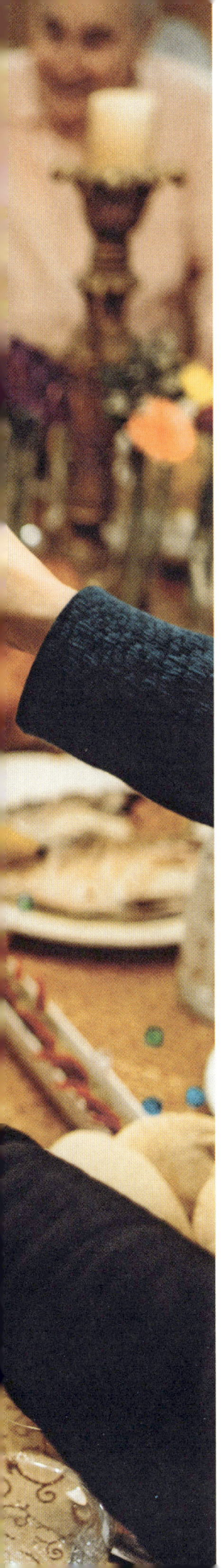

CHOLENT WITH OXTAIL

6 servings

INGREDIENTS

1.2 kg oxtail, cut into pieces
vegetable oil
300 g shallots
12 cloves of garlic
1 can (400 g) chickpeas
500 g white cabbage
500 g new potatoes
1 tbsp salt
2 laurel leaves
2 sprigs of thyme

2 tsp allspice
1 tsp grounded black pepper
2 tsp sweet paprika powder
1 tsp spicy paprika powder
800 ml vegetable bouillon
18 quail eggs
½ bunch of flat-leaf parsley
1 preserved lemon (recipe p. 41)
400 g pastrami
juice and zest of 2 lemons

PREPARATION

Sauté the oxtail pieces over a medium heat in a dash of oil until they get a crust.

Chop the shallots and the garlic. Drain the chickpeas and rinse under running water. Finely chop the white cabbage. Peel the new potatoes.

Sauté the shallots and garlic in a large pan until they begin to brown. Add the salt, laurel leaf, thyme, allspice, pepper and the two types of paprika powder and sauté for around 30 seconds. Add the oxtail, chickpeas, white cabbage and new potatoes. Pour in the bouillon and simmer over low heat for about 3 hours.

Boil the quail eggs for 2 minutes and remove the shells. Add to the stew.

Chop the flat-leaf parsley and cut the peel of the preserved lemon into fine strips. Cut the pastrami into thin slices. Finish the stew with lemon juice, lemon zest, preserved lemon peel, parsley and pastrami.

BOKER TOV GOOD M

BETE'AVON ENJO

CONGRATULATIONS BALAGA

IMA MOTH

תָּחֶא ECHAD ONE

שׁוֹלָשׁ SHALOSH

שָׂמֵחַ CHAMI

עֶבְּשׁ SHEVA SEVEN שׁ

עֶשֶׂת TE

NING SHALOM GOOD DAY
OUR MEAL MAZZEL TOV
COZY MESS ABBA FATHER
TODA RABA THANK YOU
סִיֶּתָ SHTAYIEM TWO
THREE עֶבְרָא ARBA FOR
H FIVE שֵׁשׁ SHESH SIX
הָנּוּ SCHMONEH EIGHT
HA NINE רֶשַׁע ESER TEN

צים של רינה ב

SWEETS

ARRACK CRÈME BRÛLÉE

6 servings

INGREDIENTS

440 g whipped cream
190 g goat milk yoghurt
175 g egg yolks

125 g sugar + extra sugar
85 ml arrack (strong alcoholic
beverage)

PREPARATION

Preheat the oven to 100°C.

Mix the whipped cream with the yoghurt, egg yolks, sugar and arrack using a hand mixer. Pour into 6 ramekins and place for 55 minutes in the oven.

Leave to cool. Sprinkle a thin layer of sugar over each ramekin and caramelize the top with a burner.

FRIED RICE PUDDING

4 servings

INGREDIENTS

250 ml coconut milk
250 ml oat milk
25 g cane sugar
1 g saffron
2 g ginger powder
1 g cinnamon powder
1 g cardamom powder

5 kaffir lime leaves
10 g almond syrup
10 g ginger syrup
1 vanilla pod cut lengthwise
50 g rice pudding
4 tbsp almond shavings

PREPARATION

Preheat the oven to 180°C.

Boil the coconut milk with the oat milk. Add the sugar, saffron, ginger powder, cinnamon, cardamom, kaffir lime leaves, almond syrup, ginger syrup and the vanilla pod.

Place the rice pudding in a baking dish and pour the mixture over it. Cook for approximately 1 hour in the oven.

Leave the rice pudding to cool. Remove the lime leaves and vanilla pod from the pudding and stir.

Toast the almond shavings in a non-stick pan without oil.

Serve with a fig or rhubarb compote and the toasted almonds.

TAHINI BROWNIE

For 10 brownies

Brownies are tasty, but brownies with *tahini* and coarse sea salt are even tastier! They also look very nice with their unique pattern on top.

INGREDIENTS

185 g dark chocolate
240 g butter
330 g granulated sugar
90 g brown sugar
1 vanilla pod
2 g salt

5 eggs
75 g cocoa powder
305 g flour
coarse sea salt
a few tbsp *tahini* paste

PREPARATION

Preheat the oven to 180°C.

Break the chocolate into pieces. Place in a bowl with the butter and melt using a bain-marie.

In another bowl, mix the granulated sugar and the brown sugar. Cut the vanilla pod lengthwise and scrape out the seeds. Add these and the salt to the sugar. Add the eggs and mix for 10 minutes. Stir in the melted chocolate.

Sift the cocoa powder and flour into the batter and mix with a spatula.

Line a deep baking tin with baking paper. Pour in the batter. Spoon the *tahini* paste on top and form a nice pattern with the back of a spoon. Sprinkle the coarse sea salt on top.

Bake the brownies for 25 minutes in the oven.

MALABI

4 servings

You can buy this classic dessert on every street corner in the Middle East.

INGREDIENTS

1 l whole milk
80 g sugar
70 g cornflour
2 tsp rose water

1 pomegranate
40 g pistachios
2 tsp dried rose petals

PREPARATION

Heat 900 millilitres of milk with the sugar in a heavy-bottomed pan.

Dissolve the cornflour in the remaining milk. Add this to the milk and sugar and cook for 3 minutes on a low heat, stirring continuously. Add the rose water and pour into 4 ramekins. Leave to stiffen for at least 4 hours in the refrigerator.

Remove the seeds from the pomegranate. Finish the *malabi* with pomegranate seeds, pistachios and rose petals.

ORANGE TART WITH CARDAMOM

12 servings

INGREDIENTS

5 eggs
285 g Greek yoghurt
380 g granulated sugar
5 tbsp almond powder
zest of 1 lemon
zest of 1 orange
150 g self-rising flour
200 g semolina (coarse)
2 tbsp baking powder
180 ml olive oil

FOR THE SYRUP

200 g pistachios
400 g honey
1 tbsp cardamom powder
juice of 2 oranges
juice of 1 lemon

PREPARATION

Preheat the oven to 180°C.

Place the eggs, yoghurt, granulated sugar, almond powder, lemon and orange zest, flour, semolina, baking powder and olive oil in a mixing bowl and mix with a wooden spoon.

Grease a large baking tin (33 cm long, 22 cm wide and 5 cm high) with butter and dust with flour. Pour in the batter and smooth with a spatula. Bake the cake for 25 to 30 minutes in the oven. Leave to cool completely in the baking tin.

For the syrup, roast the pistachios in a non-stick pan without oil. Add the honey, cardamom powder and the orange and lemon juice. Leave to cook for a few minutes.

Make holes in the cake with a skewer. Pour the syrup over the cake. Garnish with flaked almonds if you wish.

SWEET CHALLAH WITH FIGS AND HONEY LABNEH

4 servings

INGREDIENTS

4 slices of *challah* (recipe p. 58)
25 g butter
200 g *labneh* (recipe p. 46)
4 figs

50 ml honey
2 tbsp walnuts
zest of 1 lemon

PREPARATION

Lightly roast the *challah* slices in a pan with butter. Brush with *labneh*. Slice the figs and place on the *labneh*. Drizzle honey over it. Coarsely chop the walnuts and sprinkle over the toasts. Finish with lemon zest.

HAZELNUT CAKE WITH LABNEH AND PLUMS

4 servings

INGREDIENTS

200 g butter
140 g sugar
270 g flour
4 eggs
salt

60 g hazelnuts
150 g *labneh* (recipe p. 46)
1 tbsp honey
2 plums

PREPARATIONS

Preheat the oven to 170°C.

Cut the butter into cubes and place in the food processor bowl and mix with the K-blade at a low speed. Add the sugar.

Add an egg to the batter and mix. Then add a quarter of the flour and mix. Repeat this until you finish all the eggs and flour. Add a pinch of salt. Finely chop the hazelnuts and stir them into the batter.

Grease a springform pan with butter. Pour the mixture into the springform pan and bake for 35 minutes in the oven.

Beat the *labneh* with the honey until it's fluffy. Cut the plums into pieces.

Cut the cake into pieces and serve with whipped *labneh* and cut plums.

MANGO SORBET WITH LABNEH AND NUT & POPPY SNAPS

4 servings

Don't have an ice-cream maker? Then go looking for the best mango sorbet you can find for this delicious dessert.

INGREDIENTS

50 ml water
50 g granulated sugar
2 ripe mangos
1 tbsp lemon juice
salt
60 g butter
100 g brown sugar

50 g maple syrup
50 g flour
1 tsp cornflower
30 g mix of nuts
30 g poppy seeds
150 g *labneh*

PREPARATION

Heat the water and dissolve the granulated sugar in it. Leave the sugar syrup to cool completely.

Peel the mangoes and remove the stones. Purée the flesh in a blender with the sugar syrup, lemon juice and a pinch of salt. Mix well and place the mixture in the ice-cream maker. Turn into sorbet in 30 minutes.

Preheat the oven to 175°C.

Melt the butter. Mix with the brown sugar and maple syrup. Add the flour and cornflour. Coarsely chop the nuts and add them to the mixture with the poppy seeds and a pinch of salt.

Line a baking tray with baking paper. Place small rounds of the mixture on the baking sheet. Bake the snaps for 10 minutes in the oven. Place on a wire rack to cool.

Pour the *labneh* into ramekins. Add a scoop of mango sorbet and finish with snaps.

BABKA CAKE

For 2 cakes

INGREDIENTS

125 g whole milk
21 g fresh yeast
70 g sugar
530 g flour
6 g salt
1 teaspoon vanilla essence
zest of 1 lemon
3 g cardamom powder
4 eggs
145 g butter at room temperature

FOR THE CHOCOLATE FILLING

125 g whipped cream
110 g dark chocolate (at least 50% cocoa)
60 g dark brown sugar
20 g cocoa powder
35 g butter at room temperature
125 g praline paste or chocolate spread with hazelnuts (Nutella or the like)

FOR THE FINISHING

2 egg yolks
30 g peeled hazelnuts

FOR THE SUGAR SYRUP

65 g cane sugar
50 g water

PREPARATION

Heat the milk to 30°C and then dissolve the yeast in it.
Place the milk in the food processor bowl with the sugar, flour, salt, vanilla essence, lemon zest, cardamom powder and eggs. Knead for about 3 minutes. Cut half of the butter into cubes and add little by little to the mixture. Knead for 5 minutes at medium speed. Add the rest of the butter in the same way and knead for another 6 minutes. Cover the bowl with a clean kitchen towel and leave to rise for 1 hour.

Fold the dough from the side to the inside. Place in a square, sealed container and put in the fridge. Heat the whipping cream for the chocolate filling to just below boiling point. Break the chocolate into pieces and place in a bowl with the sugar. Pour over the warm cream and stir until smooth. Sift in the cocoa powder and mix well. Add the butter and the praline paste and mix. Leave to rest.

Divide the dough into two parts. Roll out to about 4 centimetres thick. Spread the chocolate filling on the dough and roll up as shown in the picture. Cut in half and braid the strands. Place the babka cakes in a greased rectangular baking tin and leave to rise for another hour.

Preheat the oven to 180°C.
Beat the egg yolks with a little water and brush the top of the cakes with it. Fine chop the hazelnuts and sprinkle over the cakes. Bake the cakes for 25 minutes in the oven.

Heat the water with the cane sugar. Brush the cakes with the sugar syrup when they come out of the oven.

Leave the cakes to cool for at least 30 minutes. If you cut them too soon, they might tear.

DRINKS

LIMONANA

4 servings

INGREDIENTS

1 l water
250 g cane sugar

1 bunch of mint
500 ml lemon juice

PREPARATION

Boil the water with the sugar. Once the sugar has dissolved, remove from the heat.
Cut the mint coarsely. Add the mint and lemon juice to the sugar water and mix with
the immersion blender for a few minutes.

Leave to cool. Pour the liquid through a fine sieve and serve with plenty of ice cubes.

VERVEINE ICED TEA

4 servings

INGREDIENTS

1 l water
350 g cane sugar
5 g verveine loose leaf tea (lemon verbena)
5 g samba loose leaf tea

10 g fresh mint
1 bunch of fresh verbena (lemon verbena)
600 ml lemon juice

PREPARATION

Boil the water with the sugar, verbena tea and samba tea. Once the sugar has dissolved, remove from the heat. Coarse chop the mint and the fresh verbena. Add the mint, verbena and lemon juice to the water. Mix with the immersion blender for a few minutes. Leave to cool and pour through a fine sieve. Serve with plenty of ice cubes.

ISRAELI PORNSTAR

5 servings

FOR THE RAS EL HANOUT CORDIAL

60 ml water
25 g sugar
4 g *ras el hanout* (recipe p. 36)
1 g citric acid (for food)

FOR THE PASSION FRUIT MIX

100 ml Gray Goose vodka
100 ml *ras el hanout* cordial
100 ml passion fruit juice

FOR FINISHING EACH COCKTAIL

90 ml passion fruit mix
10 ml aquafaba (the liquid from a can of chickpeas)
ice cubes
cava
2 passion fruits

PREPARATION

Heat the water for the cordial. Dissolve the sugar in it and stir in the *ras el hanout* and citric acid.

Mix the Gray Goose with the *ras el hanout* cordial and the passion fruit juice.

For each cocktail, place 90 millilitres passion fruit mix, 10 millilitres of aquafaba and a few ice cubes in a cocktail shaker. Pour through a fine sieve into a cocktail glass. Finish with a dash of cava and half a passion fruit.

SUMAGRONI

4 servings

FOR THE SUMAC MIX

100 ml Bombay Sapphire gin
100 ml Martini bitter
100 ml Martini Rubino
50 g water
2 g sumac

FOR FINISHING EACH COCKTAIL

120 ml sumac mix
ice cubes
splash of orange juice
dried orange

PREPARATION

Heat the Bombay Sapphire with the Martini bitter, Martini Rubino, water and sumac to about 60°C in a saucepan. Remove from the heat and let it rest for a few hours.

Fill a tumbler with ice cubes. Swirl around to make sure the glass is cold. Pour out the melted water.

Fill the glass with 120 millilitres of sumac mix. Add a splash of orange juice and finish with a slice of dried orange.

TEL AVIV

A CITY THAT NEVER SLEEPS

When Sinatra sang about *a city that never sleeps*, he was talking about New York, but it could have just as easily been Tel Aviv.

Israel's second largest city is not that old. It was built in 1908 near Jaffa as a garden city with beautiful homes. In the centre is a large park with all the public buildings. In the 1930s, a second wave of construction of over 4,000 buildings that followed the principles of Bauhaus and the International Style took place. This is how the city got its nickname the White City, which UNESCO named a World Cultural Heritage site in 2003.

Plan your next travel here !

'IN TEL AVIV, LISTEN TO THE LOCALS TO FIND THE BEST RESTAURANT, THE BEST CAFÉ, AND THE BEST NIGHTCLUB.'

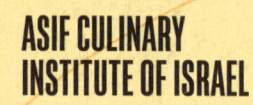

THE BEACH

Nowhere is a beach more bustling with life than in Tel Aviv. People come here to celebrate their birthday or the end of their military service. Families to picnic with their small children. Beautiful young people stroll here or play sports. There are yoga classes and waves to surf. Every beach bar serves fantastic food costing next to nothing. The place is an explosion of nationalities where you will hear every possible language. Tel Aviv beach is a place to celebrate life. Every day is a party.

ASIF CULINARY INSTITUTE OF ISRAEL

Asif has recently opened on Tel Aviv's Lilienblum Street. This is a culinary centre in the heart of the city with a cookbook library, rooftop farm, deli and eatery. Young chefs, food makers and wine producers show you what they are capable of.

SHUK HACARMEL

The Carmel market is open every day (except on Saturdays) from early morning until sunset (see p. 28). You will literally find everything there: fresh fruit and vegetables, herbs, spices, meat and fish, clothing, electronics, you name it.

OLD JAFFA

The oldest part of the city existed long before Tel Aviv was built. It extends over a hill along the Mediterranean Sea. To visit Old Jaffa is to step back in time. There is a charming marina and an old fishing port where you can see the boats moor full of fresh catch.

ROTSCHILD BOULEVARD

This beautiful pedestrian boulevard runs from the Neve Tzedek district to the Habima Theatre. You can cycle or stroll along this wide tree-lined avenue with abundant little parks where the children can romp to their hearts' content. You will also find plenty of eateries and coffee bars on Rothschild Boulevard. Many of the unique houses on the UNESCO World Cultural Heritage List are located in this street.

THE RESTAURANTS AND EATERIES

Chef Eyal Shani is a household name in Israel. This famous television chef opened his first business in Jerusalem in 1989, but now owns several Middle East-inspired restaurants worldwide—like the chic HaSalon but also the more friendly-priced Miznon chain. His signature dish, pita filled with roasted cauliflower, is a must. Feel free to visit with your kids.

The staff will take them off your hands as soon as you enter, so you can enjoy your meal quietly and without worries. Tel Aviv is actually one big restaurant full of eateries, stalls, hip coffee bars and chic restaurants. We recommend listening to the locals. They'll be happy to tell you the best places to eat at any given moment.

TEL AVIV MUSEUM OF ART

If you like modern art, this museum is a must. Here you'll find many works by international modern and contemporary artists (Klimt, Kandinsky, Chagall, Matisse...) and the largest collection of Israeli art.

TEL AVIV'S NIGHT LIFE

Tel Aviv is known for its fantastic night life, but we can't tell you where to go. The coolest parties take place in secret locations—an office building, the beach, a secluded storage shed or an open space in the city. Listen, keep your eyes open and let yourself be sucked in by the energy of the city. That's how the locals do it.

BRUSSELS - TEL AVIV

Distance: 3.245,60 km
Surface area Tel Aviv: 52 km²
Number of inhabitants in
Tel Aviv: 435,855

LAILA TOV

LAILA TOV

Sleep well. Good night. But also: enjoy your evening. These are all different meanings of laila tov and they reflect, just like *boker tov*, a piece of Tel Aviv. You never know what the city will bring you...

Laila is the daughter of the night and in this case Boker Tov's big sister. In this special restaurant on the top floor of an Antwerp office building, Tom and Lori serve you the best products and dishes from the Middle East. Everything is prepared with great respect for tradition. Similar to Boker Tov, everyone is welcome, provided they come with a common goal: to enjoy a great night out.

At Laila, Tom and Lori organize a perfect night out for their guests. Fine dining, special and sometimes exclusive drinks, a DJ in the background, beautiful views and beautiful people in a relaxed, casual setting.

But we'll tell you that story in the next book...

SLEEP WELL
GOOD NIGHT
ENJOY YOUR EVENING

TODA RABA

TODA RABA

Bedankt aan onze partners, voor het mee mogelijk maken van dit boek!

ABA & IMA

You're not only our greatest source of inspiration... You're also our inexhaustible supply of love and food. Toda raba for your endless availability for our two princesses... You almost make entrepreneurship carefree.

BIONDA

You were extraverted, queer, inclusive... You were the embodiment of Tel Aviv. You were and are our eternal source of inspiration. You are a big ball of joy, always energizing us.

FAMILY AND FRIENDS

Thanks for supporting us, for missing us, for accompanying us, for pushing us! Thanks for always being there.

BOKER TOV FAMILY

To our team, our partners... from the bottom of our hearts: YOU ARE FCKING AWESOME!!! Thank you all for your support, your smile, your flexibility... Thank you for your out of the box mentality. You are our rock stars. Keep smiling, you're on stage!

BRUSSELS AIRLINES

Thanks to Brussels Airlines, for welcoming us with a smile and make our flights easy and carefree.

BACARDI BENELUX

Pour the Bacardi Benelux spirits to make a refreshing celebration from every Purim Party.

SERAX

It's wonderful to find the colours and diversity of Tel Aviv in the Serax collections. We are very happy to serve our delicious food on their plates.

SLIGRO

Our daily delivery of fresh foods comes from Sligro. Quick and efficient, they are a great partner to work with every day!

GROWZER

We are able to finetune every recipe thanks to Growzer.

CORES DEVELOPMENT

Cores Development ensures literally and figuratively that we are able to push our restaurant Laila to the next level.

CHAUDFONTAINE

Chaudfontaine is a unique Belgian mineral water. The water travels for more than 60 years through pure rock layers and collects all sorts of minerals along the way. Then it springs at the source of the Ardens, where it is bottled. And just like Tel Aviv sparkles, we like the sparkling water best.

GOLAN HEIGHTS WINERY

Thanks you for letting us enjoy the delicious organic wines during our trip to Tel Aviv. The Yarden will remain a fixed value in our assortment at Boker Tov and Laila.

CONVERSION TABLE

Weights for dry ingredients		Liquid measures		Oven temperatures	
1g	0.04oz	30 ml	1.01 fl oz	45 °C	113 °F
5 g	0.17oz	45 ml	1.52 fl oz	100 °C	212 °F
10 g	0.35oz	65 ml	2.2 fl oz	160 °C	320 °F
15 g	0.53oz	70 ml	2.37 fl oz	180 °C	356 °F
30 g	1.06oz	100 ml	3.38 fl oz	200 °C	392 °F
100 g	3.53oz	150 ml	5.07 fl oz	240 °C	464 °F
130 g	4.6oz	170 ml	5.75 fl oz		
150 g	5.29oz	180 ml	6.08 fl oz		
200 g	7.05oz	200 ml	6.76 fl oz		
250 g	9oz	250 ml	8 fl oz		
300 g	10.58oz	260 ml	8.79 fl oz		
340 g	11.99oz	300 ml	10.14 fl oz		
420 g	14.81oz	400 ml	13.53 fl oz		
500 g	1lb 1.64oz	500 ml	16.9 fl oz		
650 g	1lb 6.9oz	800 ml	27.05 fl oz		
750 g	1lb 10.5oz	1 l	33.8 fl oz		
900 g	1lb 15.75oz				
975 g	2lb 2.39oz				
1 kg	2lb 3.27oz				

INDEX

A

allspice 36, 100, 137
almond powder 153
almond syrup 146
almonds, with skin 37
almonds, flaked 71, 72, 146
amba 50, 124
apple (jonagold) 116
apple, sour 94
aquafaba (chickpeas liquid) 168
arrack 79, 145
aubergine 93, 101, 102, 124
avocado 94

B

baking powder 105
beef, ground 100
bell pepper (yellow, red) 66
biber salcasi 41, 66
bicarbonate of soda 52
bread (Lebanese) 89, 120
brine 44, 80
broad beans (cooked) 70
broad beans (dry) 105
bulgur 90
burrata 113
buttermilk 89

C

cabbage, red 110
cabbage, white 110, 137
caraway seed 133
cardamom powder 36, 71, 72, 146, 153, 159
cardamom seed 44
carrot 44, 110
cauliflower 127
cava 168
cayenne pepper 47, 50
celeriac 116
celery 44
challah 58, 72, 76, 123, 154
chermoula mayonnaise 110, 127
cherries 117
chervil 110
chicken 44
chicken schnitzels 106, 120
chicken stock 133
chicken thighs 106
chickpeas 133, 137
chickpeas, dried 52
chilli garlic sauce 93
chilli pepper, red 41, 44, 51, 66, 70, 94, 133, 134
chocolate spread with hazelnuts 159
chocolate, fondant 149, 159

cinnamon powder 36, 72, 106, 133, 146
citric acid 52, 168
clove powder 36
cocoa powder 149, 159
coconut fat 71
coconut milk 70, 146
coleslaw 110, 120, 123, 130
coriander 51, 89, 94, 89, 94, 101, 105, 123, 127, 133
coriander powder 37, 51, 13
coriander seed 36
cornflakes 106
cornstarch 150, 156
courgette 113
courgette, Nice 133
couscous 117
cream, whipped 145, 159
crème fraîche 72
cucumbers, pickled 44, 123, 130
cucumbers, Turkish 89, 90, 94, 101, 117
cumin powder 36, 41, 47, 50, 51, 70, 90, 101, 105, 106, 133
cumin seed 36, 46, 52

D

date molasses 40
dates 40
dill 51, 80, 89, 101, 105, 117, 120, 123
dorade royale 134
dukkah 37, 130

F

fattoush salad 88, 120, 124, 134
fennel 79, 113
fennel seed 37, 44, 46
fenugreek 50
feta 76, 133
figs 154
fish sauce 94
flour 56, 59, 62, 63, 106, 155, 159
flour, self-raising 153
flowers, edible 113

G

garlic 44, 47, 50, 51, 52, 66, 70, 80, 89, 94, 100, 105, 106, 110, 113, 124, 127, 133, 134, 137
gin, Bombay Sapphire 171
ginger powder 36, 146
ginger syrup 146
ginger, fresh 94
goat cheese 75
goat cheese, hard 116

grain mustard 50
grapefruit 134
grapes, blue 116

H

harissa 41, 66, 110, 127, 130
hazelnuts 37, 116, 155, 159
honey 56, 59, 71, 110, 116, 153, 154, 155
hot dog buns with sesame seeds 130
hummus 52, 99, 100, 101, 102, 124

J

jalapeño pepper 47

K

kaffir lime leaves 94, 146
ketchup 130

L

labneh 46, 46, 154, 155
lamb, minced 100, 133
laurel leaves 44, 44, 46, 137
leche de tigre 94
leek 44
lemon 41, 70, 75, 101, 110, 127, 134, 137, 153, 154, 159
lemon juice 40, 45, 47, 50, 51, 52, 89, 90, 94, 99, 106, 110, 113, 116, 117, 127, 133, 153, 156, 164, 167
lemon pepper 52, 75
lemon pepper 90
lemon, preserved 41, 137
lemongrass stalks 94
lime 94
lime juice 50

M

mango 50, 156
maple syrup 71, 110, 156
Martini bitter 171
Martini Rubino 171
merguez sausages 130
mint 89, 90, 94, 117, 120, 123, 164, 167
miso, blond 50
mushrooms, forest 102
mushrooms, mixed 75, 102
mustard 127
mustard seed 37
mustard seed, yellow 37

N

Noilly Prat 79
nuts, mixed 156
mustard seed, yellow 37

O

oat flakes 71
oat milk 146
oil, frying 105
olive oil, smoked 113
olives 46, 101
onions (red) 89, 94, 102, 113, 117
onions 44, 66, 133
onions, silver 75
onions, spring 89, 90, 101, 105, 117
orange 71, 72, 153
orange juice 171
orange, blood 46
orange, dried 171
oregano 36
oregano, dried 46
oxtail 1377

P

panko 106
paprika powder 36, 37, 106, 110, 133, 137
paprika powder, smoked 41, 50, 66, 102
parsely 89, 123, 133
parsely, flat-leaf 51, 69, 70, 90, 99, 100, 101, 102, 105, 117, 120, 123, 127, 137
parsley stems
passion fruit 168
passion fruit juice 168
passion fruit mix 168
pastrami 76, 123, 137
peas 133
pecan nuts 71
pepper, yellow, pointed 41
peppers, Turkish green 45
pickled vegetables 44, 134
pine nuts 100
pistachios 150, 153
pita breads 89, 124
plums 155
pomegranate 72, 72, 117, 150
pomegranate juice 40
pomegranate molasses 40, 72
ponzu 50, 93
poppy seed 156
poppy seeds 156
potatoes, new 137
praline paste 159
puff pastry 75
Pul Biber 36, 75, 80, 94, 106, 110, 113, 116, 127, 133

Q

quail eggs 137

R

radishes 89, 117
rapeseed oil 62
ras el hanout 36, 66, 106, 168
ras el hanout cordial 168
rice, dessert 146
rice, unpolished 133
rose petals 36, 150
rose water 150
rosemary 44

S

saffron 146
salade fattoush 88, 120, 124, 134
salmon fillet 79
samba tea 167
samphire 113
sea bass fillet 94
semolina 153
sesame seeds 36, 37, 75
sesame seeds, white 59
shallot 45, 94, 137
silan 40
spinach 75
star anise 41, 44
sugar, cane 44, 133, 146, 159, 164, 167
sugar, dark brown, 159
sumac 36, 37, 45, 75, 89, 94, 110, 113, 117, 171
sumac batch mix 171
sunflower oil 56, 66, 106, 133

T

tabbouleh 90, 134
tahini 47, 93, 120, 123, 127, 130, 134
tahini paste 47, 50, 52, 149
thyme 44, 116, 134, 137
tomato paste, concentrate 133
tomatoes 47, 66, 70
tomatoes 89, 90, 93, 99, 100, 101, 117
tomatoes, cherry 89, 90, 93, 99, 100, 101, 117
turmeric powder 36, 37, 50, 106, 127, 133

V

vanilla extract 159
vanilla pod 146, 149
vegetable stock 94, 137
verbena (lemon verbena) 167
verbena tea (lemon verbena) 167
vinegar, natural 44, 80, 99
vinegar, red wine 41, 47
vinegar, sushi 37, 45, 94

vinegar, white wine 37, 89, 127
vodka, Gray Goose 168
walnuts 154
wine (white) 79

Y

yeast 56, 59, 62, 63, 159
yoghurt, cow's milk 46
yoghurt, goat's milk 46, 145
yoghurt, Greek 153
yuzu juice 45
yuzu vinaigrette

Z

za'atar eggs 76
za'atar 36, 37, 62, 69, 75, 117, 123
za'atar bread 134
zhug (green) 51, 76, 93, 134
zhug (red) 51, 120, 124

COLOPHON

www.lannoo.com
Register on our website and we will regularly send you a newsletter with information about new books and interesting, exclusive offers.

Concept: Tom Sas, Lori Dardikman
Recipes: Thomas Swenters
Text: Hilde Smeesters
Graphic design: Sissi Lauwers
Photography: Trix Breuls
Translation to English: Michael Lomax

If you have observations or questions, please contact our editorial office: redactielifestyle@lannoo.com

© Tom Sas & Uitgeverij Lannoo nv, Tielt, 2022
D/2022/45/95– NUR 440
ISBN: 978 94 014 8256 1

This book contains links, hyperlinks or references to websites that are not owned by Lannoo Publishers. Lannoo cannot be held responsible for the contents of the websites referred to, nor for the offers, products or services that are mentioned on these websites.